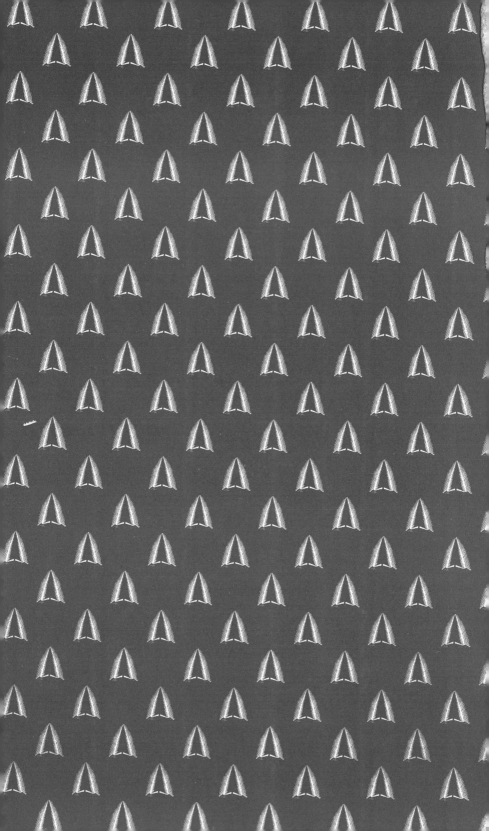

Kilmarnock

KILMARNOCK

Tony Cosier

PENUMBRA PRESS

Published by Penumbra Press with financial assistance from the
Canada Council and the Ontario Arts Council.

Penumbra Press Poetry Series Number 35
ISBN 0 921254 644

Canadian Cataloguing in Publication Data

Cosier, Tony, 1945–
   Kilmarnock

(Penumbra Press poetry series ; no. 35)
Poems.
ISBN 0-921254-64-4

1. Montague (Ont. : Township) – Poetry. 2. Rideau
Canal (Ont.) – History – Poetry.   I. Title.   II. Series.

PS8555.074K5 1994   C811'.54   C94-931123-5
PR9199.3.C67K5 1994

For Janet

ACKNOWLEDGEMENTS

The author wishes to acknowledge the help he received from
the staff of the following institutions: The National Archives
of Canada; Parks Canada; Merrickville, Nepean, and Ottawa Public
Libraries; Perth Land Registry Office; the Township of Montague.

Thanks to Alice Hughes of Easton's Corners; Al and Jean McKay
of Burritt's Rapids; Robert and Nora Nicholls of Merrickville; and
especially to Bob and Wanda McCreary of Kilmarnock for their
inspiration and insights.

Some of these poems appeared originally in the following
publications: Amethyst Review, Antigonish Review, Blueline,
Bywords, Green's Magazine, Hook and Ladder, New Quarterly,
Plains Poetry Journal, Round Table, Time of Singing, Tower,
Trail and Landscape, Voices International.

"Neighbours" received an honourable mention in the 1991 Jane
Jordan Poetry Competition.

"Running the Richmond Fen" was selected for inclusion in the
League of Canadian Poets anthology Vintage 91, published by Sono
Nis Press.

CONTENTS

Field Magic

Sometimes the beauty strikes you
In the face. You clomp with arms full of firewood
Into the upland meadow and there's the deer
Browsing grey on the buckthorn
Before it reacts, flits in a whitetailed blur
Zigzag to the fence where it's up at a blue black cloud
And down through a swallowing bough
Like a dreambeast gone.

More likely you're down on your knees
To look for it, taking in the hard way
Upside down round the edge of a crust of ice
A world of glinting crystals in a cave
Until your spine grows weary and you rise
With reluctance, leaving your vision to that last icy day
A simplest deflection of rays
Can spirit it off.

Stone

The stones of the house are sullen and do not speak .
The front stairs are cemented and wedged in sand.
The pit at the back is squared in sturdy lines.

Beyond the fence, though, picked field stones,
With even a little coaxing,
Will rub or wobble a tune
Or thunder and drum.

The shed, too, is a game one
For shifting a log with a thunk
Or clicking a bagfull of twigs
Or rattling a shiver into an eavestrough's length.

Only the pump is silent
With its handle gone
And its rusted pipe laid flat.

I think of the racket it must have made in its day
With a labourer gasping the pace
For knocks and squeaks and squeals
And all that bucketed water tumbled and sloshed.

I look to the hump that buries the site of the barn,
The heave of grass that hides the foundation stone,
And sense the diviner's urge to uncover the well,
Set the pump on end again where it stood,
Return it renewed to the earth like Antaeus
To snort the air like a wild winged horse
And plunge to the depth so profound it seems a source
To come up chilling clear, tasting of truth
That true in old John Chester's time
Still holds true today.

The halved and quartered maple blocks
Slump with a swaybacked heavy look
Weathered grey as the stile
And rails they lean on.

They make the grass look paler than it is
As it drops through poplars into snapdragon
And browning goldenrod to where the stump
Still bulks upended.

Approach the wreck one careful step at a time
As if it were an animal that could bolt.
Circle it, eyeing it, past frayed bark
And windsmoothed twistings round the angled severance

Back to bark and clumps of root
Humping thickly shoulder high
Like a blackened gritty sunflower
Loamy and full of flint.

Listen as roots like grainy chunks of wood
Split in tongues to speak.
Do nothing by halves, they say,
Take everything far as you can,

Murmuring,
All who dare to climb the sky
Must have the courage first
To go down with all their strength into the dark.

Step back to measure this marriage to earth
And prove the claim with soil
Not only grasped in the claws
But riding upward over them

In waves of sod. Notice the scurfs of lichen then,
The plantain lolling with moss,
The tangle of hay through sweetbriar
That bunches the hump in a knot.

Even empty like this, blown snow drifting where the wind
   sighs,
You can still feel life in the place.
The fork with half a handle leans as if set aside
By someone simply called away for a space.
A carriage wheel axled in white looks discontent, and drops
A shoulder to strain at its bonds of rust. Bare
Dried weedstalks puff ice crystals to cusps
And lighten the yard with charm like planted flowers.
Stand long enough and sounds begin to come. Hoof drumming
   board.
Knock on knock of maul driving trunnel through wood.
Slabs of slate begin to move, flatstep down for depth
In a conscious descent to a wall of nothing but stone
Conjured and shaped and balanced to fit on stone
And nudged right into the heart of the hill for warmth.

A leaf flicks. And a second leaf and a third.
Drizzle that all day yesterday pooled and ran in rivulets
Is settling in again to set the mood
For reaching into the closet with both hands,
Taking out the folder carefully, laying it on the table
Bulging with the deeds and wills and photographs
That so easily now can push me
Up and down a fifty acre lot,
Squinting back through time as through a mist,
Dreaming up the ghosts.

I think of William Fortune
Forcing a path through thicket and thorns
To plot his chains on a grid.
He pencils it down.
Johnstown. Montague.
Lot twenty-one. Concession one.

John Chester is first to stay. A Loyalist.
Burned out in Albany, 1763,
Trading cows and hogs,
What was once a quiet life,
For swamps and Sherwood's Rangers,
A limp from a ball in the foot.
By 1781, completely an exile,
Bivouaced at Saint John's,
Begging food from the Commissariat,
Drawing his lot from a hat.
He poled a batteau against the Saint Lawrence
To Brockville, carted overland north
To somewhere not here,
Here only in 1801.

A lay preacher by then.
Pathmaster. Farmer. Timber runner.
Builder of Chester's Bridge.

Husband to Phoebe. Father to
Hannah and Polly and Elizabeth
Michael and Thomas and Harriet and Jessie
And, after the death of an infant John,
To John,
Risen like the Phoenix,
So much like his father
The two fused, became inextricable,
A Loyalist colossus
Lingering nearly two centuries.

A contract barely legible
Tells me Chester sold to Kennis Brannick
For a hundred pounds
On the second of May one thousand eight hundred and forty-
    one
and opened a new chronicle.

Brannicks this time.
Good Catholic neighbours to the township,
Stable in a world that dropped like a stone
Hellbent day and night through the steamboat frenzy
And the railway surge.
Devils for work, Brannicks kept at everything Chesters had
    begun,
Cleared more bush, picked more stones,
Sowed and harvested,
Cut the ice, boiled the sap,
Tended the animals.
Behind the horse and then upon the tractor,
They plowed a steady furrow fifty years.

Moirs brought the property into the next century
And took it halfway through.
A prolific lot, with so many tendrils branching
To so many farms and homes,

Not even a Moir could tell exactly
Who lived in what house when.
The old patriarchs, John, then James, then Robert,
Parcelled out their holdings
A dozen ways each time they wrote a will
And when wills were not enough
Went back at them again with codicils,
Scattering tables and chairs with colts and heifers
Through the kingdoms of their choosing
Like Anglo-Saxon chiefs bestowing rings.

The last of the Moirs to own the strip
Was Essie,
Who lived a whole life here.
Seventy years, longer than five succeeding owners were to
    reside.
If there is a ghost to haunt this lot,
It will be Essie Maitland Moir's,
Though who can guess what shape that soul will take?

Will she return the aged spinster
Cursed by the blessing of Robert Moir,
Who willed his daughter "a home in the dwelling
On above devised lands so long as she remains single"?
For single she stayed,
Though becoming a mother of sorts,
Steadying keel to her brother's children,
Smoothing the panic out of their troubled lives
With the same calm with which she penned a letter
In a graceful hand, so gently without a trace of bitterness
The marker on her gravestone links her with that charity
And names her Auntie Essie.

Or will her spirit hold to a younger form
The way her living bones could not,
Retaining the trim lines of the swimmer,
Climber of trees, rider of horses,
Who will slide quiet and beautiful to us
Out of the attic, the bookcase, wherever she hides,
To find the familiar corner
Where the old Dominion prevails,
Settle before it softly as a bird upon a nest,
Turn her profile, arch her back,
Lock her wrists in the old high wristed style
And stroke the keys to fill us
Slowly and steadily note by tender note
The way a whole pond fills with drops of rain;
And when the sun comes back,
Take our spirits with her out
To greet the day with the cone flower and Queen Anne's lace,
Tangible and telling as the odour of mint
Or the lift of the whirring meadowlark.

He was not one to let an emotion show,
Unless an obvious bitter one
With a cuff at the ear of a horse
Or an oath at a backbreaking stone.

But the care he would take to cut a block of ice
And slide it from the river in a piece

Spoke up from his boots
Through his curving knees and his back
As he sat by the fire at night
With a knife and a handsized block

Working the shape and the lines
Controlled and calmly in.

He beaked his dove, curved its head,
Tucked in the talons, rounded the eye.
He feathered wings so exactingly
They could almost stretch and fly.

He hummed as he worked, and was patient; but once he was
    done,
He was out of his depth again.

He was up restless and fidgeting,
Looking for someone, Grover, Cyril, anyone
He could give the thing to
And call it done

With "Here!" and the gift extended
And no other word.

My brother drew the whetstone one last scrape.
My father took a finger across the blade, confirmed it
And passed the scythe to me.

They led me to the field
And took it back for two swathes each.
Snick snick. Snick snick.
Then one positioned the handle in front of me
While the other angled my wrists square on the nibs.

The rest of the morning and all of the pasture were mine –
That much they made clear
Before they went back to sharpen the hatchet and froe.

I swung the scythe through the air a practice swipe,
So pleased with myself I forgot
How the long edge hooked as I snapped it back
And almost sliced a thigh.

I stood still at the corner after that,
Eyeing up the slope I had to climb,
Trying to imagine the spot
Where I'd probably tumble myself
So small and thin and lost in grass
They'd have to mow it to find my whitened bones.

With no choice but to begin it, I began:
Carefully stroking the blade away from me.
Though once I got well into it I was fine.
Hay crackled over the sweep as though it were skipping a rope
And settled smooth as sleep, as if it understood
It wouldn't be lying long but stooked and up again,
Fed back into life all winter
To follow a circuit into the guts of cows
And back to the field once more,

Stacked and spread and steaming
Down to soil and next year's growth.

I cut my way to the hilltop and back down,
Then up and down again before I paused.
I listened to the others riving shingles.
I looked at some perky sprigs
That bristled up under my cut.
I tried to measure all that was left to do
By lifting it with the eye
And dropping it into the short grass side.
I wanted to get it finished.

That was all. How could I foresee
Eighty fields just like it I would mow,
Or think of my blistering hands
As the first small sign of inevitable wounds,
So much unending fatigue, responsibility, and doubts.
Or that I would eventually see him after all,
The grinning bonelike man,
As little more than a dot at the far end
But coming, swinging a stroke
Almost the mirror of mine
As he reaped on down my row.

I never stitched a single thing sat still.
All of it moved about on somebody's back,
Rolled around in a bucket, hoarded grain, covered a table,
Somehow got weathered down to the threadbare stock.

I kept a style, scratchy, raw like pipesmoke,
One straight quick slug of Kilborn rum,
Basic bare indeed, though it had a look.
But don't start thinking any of it was fun.

Little wheel, big wheel, flax, wool were the same,
Stirring piss in the cup, swingling, hackling, thwacking,
Never knowing where you were going until it was done
For anyone to pick at and see where you went wrong.

My own quilt has a name – Hard Row to Hoe.
Cover me with it when I'm gone and tuck it well.
The world's a hard cold place, and don't I know.
The next one will be harder and colder still.

Today I got so mad I could have screamed,
But Kennis was so far back past the brush
You couldn't hear his axe for maple bush.
What good would it have done to make a sound?

Horse and chickens wouldn't care what I felt,
And noone else that could care was in view.
So I gave in, resolved the thing to do
Would be to come inside and set the quilt.

It's only cloth on cloth with stuff between,
A woman's sentimental household game.
But even before I slowed beside the frame
And stroked a hand through it, I knew I was softening.

Just looking at three orange blooms was nice;
Thinking about the little one coming was bliss.
Four tulips, four girls – a mother can bless
The treasures of her home in secret ways,

Powerfully as any angel, with love enough
And time. I'm turning the flowers upside down around
Like a spinning wheel that goes down at my hand
And always predictably, buoyantly comes back up.

I'll teach my girls resilience with that. And Kennis
Will like it. He loves to see a balanced thing work out.
He chops, mows hay, plants his field that way.
Knowing him, he'll chuckle at what I was riled about.
That is, if I still remember what it was.

Hard miles past any settlement,
He thanks the tricks that take him through the storm
And keeps on pushing north.

The pressure of the Book inside his vest
Keeps his memory edging into the Testament,
Shapes the words of the Psalms so well
He almost sings aloud.

The darkest path has comforts,
He tells the horse and himself
As he looks to the twisted knot of boughs
Sheltering them from the hail.

At a log bridge full of openings
Enough to snap a leg,
He praises the wonder of the beast
That carries him over water
The way Saint Christopher mildly shouldered the cherub of
    God.

As the trail winds up through granite,
He recalls the Knight in a woodcut.
He thinks of Dante's precipice
And lifts himself, himself like his own eagle,
With a dream of another day:

A Lord's Day
With sunlight in a clearing full of folk.
A rugged lot, sinewy as cedars they've cut and cleared,
Solid as stones they've picked,
Yet still with softness in them
And great needs.

He stands in his dream

With the Book he has brought
To be the central focus for them all,
From the child just out of a mother's hands
In its first split stance,
Through clumps of mothers and daughters, fathers, sons,
Scattered up the pasture,
To the far diminished gentleman
Wavering in the shadow of his atheistic dark.

STONE HOUSE

1. SHADOW

When I think the house may not exist, that

where the thick of the forest gives way
to hills rolling into hills
out into clouds and blue,

Janet has climbed the split rails
to where the topbar nudges
in a wedge of uprights

and nestling, pointing her nose at the sun,
closed her eyes
and dreamt the place,

I root it back in the earth

with a slanting look to the river,
to the silo curving and the island's hump,
the bridge with its white kingposts at the lock.

I bend for a poplar tassel
red with pollengold
to take inside.

Before I touch the door
I stretch a hand past the frame
and feel my shadow warm upon the stone.

2. SHAPINGS

From a distance,
the house appears
a single block
tidily wider than high.

Nearer,
the rubble
shapes itself

with original mortar
muddy orange
under grey

and thick squared quoins.

Ridges of limestone
heave over
and under
granite chunks.

Pink seams intertwine
with glints of mica flakes.

Pockholes hint
that a blackish slab
bubbled up
through the core of earth

slumbered under saltwaves
for thousands of years

and only two centuries back
knew the air's first bite

when someone with a mattock
chopped and chipped it

out of soil

to hang it here
in the wind.

3. ARCH

Like so much that seems magical
the ability of stones to stand on end
is based on fundamental laws
gravity and their own weight:

wood and glass beneath them
knowing they will not fall
can rise squareshouldered in the entranceway
with confident balancing.

4. WOOD

More than
clusterflies and ants
and spiders flitting for the corners
keep up the life of the place.

The wood itself keeps breathing.

Squarenailed floor planks
shrink and open gaps
into dustier undergrain.

Wainscot and bookcase
edge away from corners.

The door to the basement,
inches short at the base,
lets bedrock shadows sift upward
through light from above streaming down.

Outside comes in the same way.
Rungs pulled in from the bush
climb grey and licheny
half a high wall to nowhere.
Firewood under a window
is piled for an exit in smoke.
A birdcage of spindly matchwood
makes an empty, delicate foil
to the heavy home-framed box
we've chained to a backyard bough
and packed to the rafters with seed,
tapered to yield every grain
for squirrel or jay or chickadee, starling
whatever bobs at its base.

Recessed into the panelling
from eye level
up to a height
beyond my reach

a puzzling domestic cave
tunnels to interior rubble
and a sleeve of brick.

A wooden frame within it
houses a bowl rounded inward
marked by gaping holes
that once nailed something in.

Was this a cradle
for a clock
that time outran?
A backdrop for a Mother Mary
or a blessing bishop in robes?
Was this a nest
that heralded a household's faith
with a saviour on a crucifix?

I ponder on what to make of it
now. A block with saints in bas relief
cut by my brother Greig?
A full figure of an angel
risen like a green shrub
out of Sibbald's bench?

Something I could work myself
into a crude chip from the woods –
a raw red cedar mask;
perched and crosswinged maplehawk;
basswood buck antlered and polished
round as a goatsbeard tuft?

As I think of these,
standing beneath the slot
or seated in a chair looking up to it

it teases with so many possibilities
opens with so much invitation

I sense in its potential
almost the inevitable comfort
of the thing already done.

6. BEAMS

With the same concentration the stones use
to grip the exterior tight
with gathered pressure downward
all the way to bedrock,
thirteen titans in the basement
bunch their massive shoulders
to force the interior up.

They are equal to the weight
and seem fresh to the task,
as if the adze that squared their sides
had nicked them only yesterday.

While shifting generations overhead
have swept with fiddlefoot, bustled to and fro,
erected walls and flattened them,
these founding beams have kept the original aim,
supported every change with equanimity.

One at the edge is coughing dry dust down
and two are charred with marks from an ancient fire,
but true to their stoic breed
they keep a gigantic chestiness.
They are taut to the hand
and bark back tight pitched at a knock.
They will not waver their lift.

juts like a beehive off the north east edge,
as if the mason deliberately lumped it out,
the way a seamstress will stitch a flaw
into a precious quilt.

Taut as the bump of a knot,
it grants the assembly uniqueness
even as it locks it finished
into an austere press.

It may have been set for extension,
a blunted loaf to build new stonework on,
first step in a dance to prove
only a house this sturdily built can spin

as it blossoms out of stoney eaves with wasps
flicking and bouncing all down the same warm side
that sprouts at its base with the earthsnake
pointing its perfect head.

8. INHERITOR

I grip both ends
of a stone
the plow has hooked
from the earth
and as I lift
I let my eye
slide toward the house
where it fits
between elm and oaks
so naturally against the sky
it seems it has always been there
and feel in the pull
of one large stone
a sense of all the weight
of all the stones
that have made the house what it is.

Consciously balancing
knees to spine
in my turning toward the grass
I think of the concentration
that must have sustained
the wisdom of 1820
as the mason
founded on bedrock,
cut the soil and laid the lines
so entrance and paired windows would face the sun.
Judged each stone
top, bottom, one best face.
Broke what needed to be broken
along the natural grain
by lightly steadily rhythmically
tapping along a mark
until the lulled rock split with a yawn .

And then built wide. Two thick walls wide

with a rougher wall between.
Shaped stone to stone,
shaped even the mortar to stone.
Built scaffolds strong enough
he could walk the length of the wall
and climb for thirty feet
carry tools and planks, buckets, wedges, rocks
without a shudder
in all weathers.
Moulded beams to joists
like the bones of a skeleton
with care. Built chimneys and eaves
with the same painstaking intensity.
Slanted roofbeams
edge to edge at the top
and rived and shingled the lot.

I work my way slowly
up and over a mound
past the rotted stoneboat
and descend to a pile of stones
where I ease my burden
not quite randomly
flat to a wide flat mate
so snugly no one would know it
the last stone placed
by the last of so many
who have cleared the field.

New to the place
not quite a farmer yet
but becoming one
I resolve to go even farther
take on some of the craft
of mason and carpenter.
A summer to lift and resettle
the stones of the front steps.
Some months of steering drainage,

pointing, shoring joists.
A summer afternoon
to mount a ladder
far as the old scaffolding
to nail down shingles
where shingles have lifted and flown
all the way up the slope
to the base of the lightning rod
where I can lean at the chimney top
look out over river and island
pasture and meadow and maple line
and feel within myself
a hawklike proud inheriting
keeper of the house.

On the wheel of the old lumber cart
The circular hub is mortised for spokes
That fan out to felloes
And form rounds within rounds.

Elliptical in the hayfield,
Stems of trefoil spin
With daisies and fleabane cilia
In a ring where the deer bedded down,

As if nature conspired with the artisan
To go back with the ancient astronomers,
Frame cycles to epicycles in unending accord
And keep Earth at the centre of things.

Except that on one of the wheels
The felloe has rusted and split
And is falling away;

A hawk has curved too close to a hedge
– Stutters out flustered with kingbirds nipping;

Swallows flick at the field
In dips and feints and flips and ripostes;

Heads of haytops twist and ripple erratically;

As the slant sun in a whipping wind
Tears at a ragged cloud.

To anyone else it would be junk.
We call it treasure,
Line our walls with wood decay and rusted metal
The way birds build a nest.

Most of it's in chunks,
Some so weirdly forged
We have no idea how they fitted
To do whatever they did.

A pewter pot's identifiable
Though no one's going to pour
From a spout that's a ragged gash.
The same holds true for a crock
All lichen beard with holes,
And a milk can stained with oil
That's long outsoured its milk.

The shovel on the other hand's a toss-up
Whether to use and chance a snap
Or lean resigned through the ladder
By the massive bow saw's teeth.

A milking stool's the only piece we've bought.
(Friends gave us the bas cul.)
The rest we've combed from the property,
Peeled off matted grass
Or scrabbled out of dirt
Like nuggets not only valuable,
Symbolic of other treasures,
Things we have not found yet,
Or have found and left to stay:

Bicycle wheels
Rims of buried buckets

Hinges Spikes
Boards of a barn so old
We can shred them in our fingertips.

These relics are sentient.
The walls of the hermit's shed,
Flattened and overgrown ,
Breathe better when we're about,
Push up posts, handles, harness
They would not want us to miss.
The harrow – a great discovery –
Lodged in moss and glacial rock,
Yipped and jumped and joggled
When you lifted it;
Bounced all the way home on my shoulder,
Happy as a springfooted fox.

The first kill, furred and red and final,
Brought more than October chill
Through the wind that sliced the crosses of our farthest fence.

The next was colder still
Where November's path slipped through the thorn
At pasture's end.

Recently, death
Closed the gap
Where pasture begins.

Now as we approach year end
Foxclaws prick the snow
On our front lawn.

Last night, near midnight,
A quick black flap of wings
Against the moon

Led me to seek
In the first blunt
Glow of morning

Scratch marks under the lilac,
Drops like shattered berries,
The familiar lament of fur.

"Wolves?" Jack says.
Four thousand miles away
I hear him gulp.
"You have wolves on your property?
Well, you'd better get a gun then."

I remember Letty fresh from the Philippines
Wading the summer alfalfa
Picking seeds from every flower
Outward on, inquisitive, very happy
Until I mentioned the fox.

And we ourselves reluctant to accept
The massive print and tree marks
Of the bear.
Not here, we say. Not so close.

A boy might take a stick to give him confidence,
A large one he can lay with left and right,
Like an armored knight with a broadsword.
Most of our farmers, like Jack, have rifles.
The stranger who left us an arrow
Carries a crossbow into his waste lands.

Still, I think,
Faulkner's timeless story advises best.
Young Ike McAslin
Following Sam Fathers' lead
Has it right.

Follow them, I tell myself,
Follow Ike and Sam
Into the Big Woods.

Not enough to look at a map

And see you're in bush already,
Gloating over miles of Marlborough Forest north and east
With Limerick Forest stretching widely south
Acres of Tay Marsh west and beyond them
Lakes and outcrops well past Foley Mountain.

You must step in
Body and soul
Alone.
Pare yourself down
To naked wits.
Walk
Past fencegap
Field
Thorn hedge
Birch
Ash
Stone cairn.
Slow.
And slower.
Stop outright.
Silent.
With earthstars.
Moss. And lichen.
Take things in.

Settle with log and rock
As light comes orange
Reddens
Purples
Greys
And quenches
Until you begin without even knowing it
To think of wolves packing and circling behind you,
Think of the hawk that you turned once to find
Hovering absolutely without sound
Behind your neck,
Imagine a misting spirit shouldering in

Half shaped emergent looming
To test you,
Sound your depths,
Curling around and into you
Enough of fear to bring perspective, truth,
Courage you could not know otherwise.

I

Chilling October bite, enough of a gust
To make a leaf fall upward, raises a limb
In the path ahead and exposes a quick grey
Wraith within the thicket's duller grey.
I hope for a deer, but it is nothing alive,
Only a heap of stones piled years ago.
Viburnum twines over it. Moss is softening an edge.
Saplings are pushing through. It is not a wall,
Not even a half wall like the one farther back
Composed of blocks so uniformly huge we've called it
The work of giants. Nor does it have the Stonehenge
Look of other crafted piles. It divides
Nothing, supports nothing, takes the eye
Nowhere. Still, it has its own impressiveness,
Telling so much the way it does so quietly.

II

Slate, conglomerations, lumps vesicular as honeycombs
Offer insights beyond the human scale.

In a thick blue shelf I recognize marks
I've seen in bedrock where deep clefts carved

North-south under thin ones lined east-west
Chronicle the scouring of the Wisconsin glacier.

Granite cracked like an eggshell along a line of pink
Suggests a story older still – ages of calm erosion

Startled by jets melted in fierce core fires
And rocketed exploding through miles of fissured crust.

49

III

Today, strange as it may seem,
These ancient rocks are my contemporaries
More than the people who piled them.
For though I see everywhere
Signs of how the old families
Toiled at picking stone
And stone and more stone
From barn yard, sheepfold, pasture, road,
And though I can imagine,
Looking on rotted remains
Of stone boats and lumber wagon,
How they teamed with horses or oxen
To drag the load,
Those farming generations are gone, every one,
As I shall be gone, and every person I know
While these rocks
Remain.

IV

When Dollier and Bréhant found a man of stone
Observing the portage at Lake Michigan, they hammered it into fragments
And drowned the broken bits. It was 1670.
They were priests. And mapmakers.
They had paddled the lakes from the Saint Lawrence,
Believing it a channel conveniently carved by God
For plundering Cathay. They were wrong.
And wrong about the Iroquois.

V

In open field, or swamp, or highland ridge,
The forest teaches again and again –
The tree that cuts its roots
Too thin in its soil
Goes down.

VI

I could build a compact dome
With an eye in its side
For putting a lantern in.

I could take a thick wide chunk
And lay a smaller on it
And then a smaller
And a smaller
After.

But they would be decorative only,
However crudely disguised.

The deep truth will not be pushed.

The figure I need in stone
Is there already,
Formed by an ancient hand
In the trees beyond the stone pile.
The day I know
The spirit in these woods
Finally well enough
To recognize it as it is,
It will come to me
Of its own accord,
The way these first stones have.

River

Say the name Kilmarnock
And I hear it slower than you say it,
Thinking of the long slow pump of the heron's wing
As it lifts off a stump that's weathered stillwater
Since the dam filled the bay last century.

Maitland's Rapids then.
A ribbon of river
Taking a bend
Past Maitland's house –
A little savage slice
Of a rift in a hurry;
Now the gentlest spot on the whole Rideau,
Meandering nearly backwards through orchard and pasture
With Kilmarnock Island and the lift beyond the dam
Barely a contour line on either side.
A poising place, with hardly a foot in its fall,
Canal and lock almost a level
Between two broad flat ponds.

The beaver swims his rounds here
Friendly as a farmhand
Yawning with the stirring birds
And the moan of cows.

Lilies float alongside
Arum and cattail.
Bees to them come lazy, gilded gold
From goatsbeard, mallow, morning glory.

Teals and mallards
Glide the flow
Or tailtipped, nonchalantly
Bob for trout.

Seasons turn more softly in such a place,
Lean into one another and slide together.
Snow geese watched on winter ice
Blend in the mind with apples flowering
And moonlight over hay.
Summer evenings full of sounding frogs
Are ghosted with lychnis, fireflies,
Tiny points of the Dipper breasting a ripple's spread.

The ignorant think there's nothing in a swamp,
That every one's the same dead trees and stink.
What would the muskrat think of that,
That lives its life in a swampy acre
Never more than yards from where it was born

And never stops observing, even as it forages
With tenacity it learned from the pygmy shrew,
Or paddles between its beavery head
And snakelike tail, or jumbles a song
It stole from a chickadee crossed with the tone of a frog.

It misses nothing, piles debris for a home
Exactly on a margin not exact
That if too high will drown a muskrat out
Too low will leave it prey for mink.
It learns a desperate wisdom as it waits

And keeps its faith, foraging, piling,
Adapting, long as it lasts.
With enough generations studying the floating moon
Or stars straight up above it through the reeds
Some night, I swear, it will glow like a firefly.

Peering through clustered reeds
between the stakes of a lodge
and a calculated tangle of dam,
I caught a glimpse of mapled height
and arced a path toward it.
As I climbed the vantage point,
a pair of geese
great winged, gigantic
of a size I had thought extinct,
squawked past my twisting shoulders,
flapped, circled and
descended with a skim
well out on beaver water.

Agents of change,
the swimming rodents
gnaw and mastermind
a life beyond their own
for more than ducks and geese,
for more than hummingbirds and herons,
more than the moose and the shrew,
more than the duckweed, tadpole, larva, dragonfly, rush,
more...

You, who would love a beaver pond,
who lament if you see a sliced tree hung in the air,
who can read the water splitting like an open book
before a swimming snout,
help me to trust
the changing way of things.
When I look at our flourishing trees
and fret at how easily beavers could destroy them,
teach me hope and countermeasures,
lead me to the ridge
above the spring pools

to sod that we will
sever, wedge, and plant
with seedling after seedling
of white pine, white spruce,
white cedar so slowgrowing
it could last four hundred years.

Clear in snow where your bootmark cleaves through mine
the clawed print of a coyote
proves the animals like to use our trails.

The way we cut cross country
following the deer path happily
until it vaults the fence rail
and leaves us chesting the bleached wood
pursuing the flight with our eyes alone
thinning into the birch.

A people walked here once
without a need for fencing.
Meanderers.
Earth treaders
who followed the sun and the ways of the moon
like tides

a people akin to the deer and wolf
that slipped through woods and fields
leaving no more sign
than a canoe will leave in a current
except for maybe an ochred shell
or stone adze with a chipped edge
Ancient Woodland learned from Clovis
way off on the margin of Agassiz
ten thousand years before
Nawacamigo
Antenewayway
Wabakeek
Shewitagan
Nawaquarkicom

and nine other Mississaugas
each with his own totem

for two pounds ten shillings a year
signed away to His Majesty
ten million seven hundred and forty-eight thousand acres
that no man ought to own.

1. MAITLANDS RAPIDS 1826
THE COMMITTEE

Maitlands Rapids distant from By Town 54-1/2 miles, and from Merricks Mills 8-1/4 miles are 186 yards in length, descent in that distance two feet 2-1/2 inches, and depth of water over the site where it was proposed to construct a Dam one foot.

The plan was to place a Lock of 4.9 feet lift in a natural snie, 440 yards in length, situated on the Right Bank of the River. A Dam of eight feet in height, average length 276 feet, and thickness sixteen feet, was to be built across the River at the head of the Rapids, to give five feet depth of water over the Upper Sill of the Lock.

2. THE PLAN 1827
EDWARD W. THOMPSON, CONTRACTOR

So there's no more talk of Irish Creek.
We go from here straight up the Rideau
through Smiths Falls into the lakes
and that makes sense.

Why gouge a ditch for miles into swamp and boulder
when you can drop by both forks off the summit
and let water do the cutting.
The Colonel has it right.
By Town to Fort Henry
all the way from the Grand
to the Garden of the Spirit
go with lakes and rivers
and drown out every rapids with a dam.

Here at Maitland's it's only a nudge of a lift,
less than a man can take up in a stride.
The width at the dam's hardly the toss of a rope
and the cut's in a natural snie.
The plan's for fifty locks
that will stretch for over
fifty miles each way
and we may have the first one licked.
But I make no promise, not yet.
You can plot it out on a map
or pace it through the bush a dozen times,
you never know what's under until you dig.

3. THE SURVEYS 1826–1827
JOHN MCTAGGART, CLERK

Our first try from the Entrance Valley
we bogged in muck so deep
we turned back to wait for frost.

With freeze-up came the snow.
The pines congealed so thickly
we hacked our way with an axe.
We could barely see for a level.
The theodolite stiffened and locked.

July brought flies and heat.
At Burritts we came to thunder and heavy rain.
We dropped a pack in a pool.
Changing places in the canoe, we overturned.
Every portage it was brambles and slipping stones.
We lost the channel in the Drowned Lands
for a day and a night
and drove a stump through the hull.

Impossible country!
No settlements. No paths.
Black tangled forest on every side.

How could anyone
push a canal
through this?

4. CLEARING THE WAY 1827
EDWARD THOMPSON, CONTRACTOR

A month ago, there was only Maitland here
on what was Maitland's land
with no one for company
but a few straggled Loyalists
hidden away in the woods
so deep only he knew where.

But now he's granted back
a slice of his tract
he's got the whole Sapper's carnival,
trappers, raftsmen, voyageurs,
every farmer's son for eighty miles
and half of Ireland.

They grub with brushhooks
and picks and hoes.
They blast with powder.
They dig. They hammer at stone
over the squeal of cables
and roaring pumps.
They shout at oxen
and one another.

Tree by crackling tree,
they fell the timber,
and pile the slash in towering heaps
to burn.

In the smoky yellow circle
of the only lamp still going
with licks of half light flickering
on our own shapes as they moved

and the darkness full of bodies
all around us sleeping,
circle within circle within circle
he took the scroll and set it on the table.

He flattened the peeled edge for me to see
and opened it outward slowly.
Shape by shape the figures he'd created
with his own teeth stood and walked.

First the bear.
Then its track.
Then the otter through the entrances
under the spell of the Four Winds and the Sun .

"This one is Meshipisshi,"
he whispered as he pointed
at a lynx with horns of a buffalo
and a tail like a curving spear,

"The Lion of the Water, much like
the Lion that floated in the wind
on the Durham boat
over the head of Colonel By.

"My Shaking Tent. Do you understand?"
I didn't. What man can look
into another's naked soul?
But I told him that I thought I did.

He tightened his scroll back then,
tied it with a string,
padded back into the darkness where I heard him
fumbling with the bundle

by the boots beside his axe.
Then he twisted into the bunk. He was tired.
So were we all after fifteen hours of grubbing in the earth
and fifteen more tomorrow to look forward to.

6. ENGINEERING THE LOCK
LIEUTENANT WILLIAM DENISON, R.E.

And of course you need six feet
of water over the sill
to account for fluctuations
in the runoff.

Now, if we go for wood,
remember if we keep it under water
it will be as strong as stone.

We'll lay squared timbers down in grooves and adjust them
to carry sleepers,
lag a frame to the sleepers
and pack it with stone chips.
We'll still need our two foot wall of
puddled clay.
Otherwise, we're in for seepage and a lot of grief.

If, on the other hand, we reach
what can be blasted to a bare rock floor,

you realize we'd need to anchor
an oak sill in by fox bolts.
We could lay it like a bin
on its side triangular
filled with rubble roughly dressed
and jointed with ...

Well, Mister Wellington, Sir,
as you will clearly notice
I've double scratched the angle
of the breastwork of the lock
so well you could set your royal compass by it.

And Mis-ter Sandby, here for you's a
pert purposive Woolwich differentiation
between the end of a roofedge and the wave of riverbend
and I guarantee, sir, when I mix my paints
I'll colour your Woolwich contrasts into it.

But that's it for the ordinance.
The rest is mine.

As it should be, gentlemen
when it's Burrows himself
who's paddled the miles
soaked and scraped and sunbaked
to the site,
Burrows who after the project's done and
every other soldier's back in England
will be staying in his old log cabin here,
John Burrows, who loves this land
and will show it that he loves it
as he draws,

stretching the lovely crosslines in the trees and overstating
    them
with figures to ply a paddle or twist at a winch if I will,
before I soak in shady and oversized and with exquisite care
a schooner with full sail bellying
so thin you can see bank and trees on the other side
and feel the water and the wind right through it as it slides.

The rider in from the Long Bush
supports what came through Wolford all last week,
what we'd all been fearing all along.

Malaria.
From the Isthmus right down the Cataraqui
Scything a swathe through the lot.
Labourers, masons, soldiers all sick again.
Clowes, who laid out the line,
is dead this time.
And Chaffey, the first miller.
The Colonel himself is down,
his own confirmation of all he denied last fall
as he shuffled in replacements for his dead.

Our farmers will be slipping home for sure.
The bush that coughed up the Canadiens
will swallow them back once they hear.
Only the Irish with nowhere to go will stay –
poor bastards – and think about the swamp they've settled in.

Swamp Fever.
Sappers claim it comes from India
but we don't need India.
Cranberry Marsh will do.
The River Styx,
With its Drowned Land
stagnant in a labyrinth of stumps,
tangled roots that drift and interlock
with floating weeds and moss and slime,

morass of poisonings,
of snakes and water rats,
a devilish land of no horizons
only lines of bonewhite spars

with herons in the notches hatching death.

There's a blue scum over Cranberry Marsh
that rides the edge at Maitlands.
The mist that lifts when the blue's disturbed
is spreading its stench around us now
exuding from the pit that we've cut open
twisting a noxious chain down the line of the lock.

EDWARD THOMPSON, CONTRACTOR

The sun's lifted far enough
to see the ferry
moored on Maitland's side.
No one has come over yet.

No one will have crossed the bridge
at the end of the island either.

I'd expected trouble of a noisier sort.
This is only silence.
Or almost silence
with only a fly buzzing,
and gulls that squawk a long way off,

the river rippling
over stones and weed
as it has for hundreds of years.

The smell is everywhere.
The noisome stench of the pit
stinking thick like a Black Death.

But I will not give in to it.

The whole length of the site
there's nothing that could be carried
not a mallet, not an axe.
The bunkhouse stretches inert
smokeless and barred
but I'll have them out of there
if I have to split it like a dead log full of ants
and spill them out.

We'll chop the trees again,
a wider gap this time,

create a wind to funnel the foul air out
and dig again
straight from the lock
right to deep water
blasting through the bedrock all the way.

10. CELEBRATION 1831
JAMES MAITLAND

Not every day
you climb to a deck
with every horn of the '67
tooting celebration
and muskets firing
and cannon roaring
and two lines of redcoats
splitting a gauntlet right to
Colonel By
who grips your hand in a doubled crush
and says, "Well done, Well done,"
as if you were the one
who'd come by steam
up from Kingston through the Narrows
down nine locks to
here.

What can you do but
shake with your own two hands
and look the man back in the eye
take in the face you will always remember
hawklike
somehow holding the rage
pretending not to know
what he of all people must know
that Merrick
eight miles on
– for Sly drowned out
and Brewer destroyed
and Chaffey ruined and dead –
has exacted his miller's revenge
and dammed the river dry.

11. ESTHER 1836
COLONEL ELIAS DURNFORD, ROYAL ENGINEERS

On the last pilgrimage to Frant, I did not see the Colonel.
I stood with Esther at St. Albans in the churchyard.

"John gave so much to Upper Canada ..."

"... it killed him," I finished for her,
remembering how he'd brushed the surgeon back
and risen from bed to guide me through the works.

"But he could not forgive his England,"
she kept on, persistent in her own way,
just like him,
and finished it herself this time,
"and that killed him a little, too."

He had dreamed of knighthood
and been granted disgrace,
a Treasury Minute that called him
fractious and incompetent.

"It broke his heart.
He visited no one.
He was too sick to attend the Inquiry.
Letter on letter he wrote defending himself."

I'd seen the desk he'd set up
at a window over a garden.
Better than Cranberry Marsh, he'd suggested.
But I thought it a sorry exchange for the Chaudière.

And his frail shape as he stooped
far from the frame that stunned his voyageurs
as he pushed their boat through the jaws of the Rideau wind.
Or walked, not ran, but walked
off the dam at Hog's Back

while it crumbled to nothing behind him
talking as he went of how he'd
build it back again.
As he did.

In his final letter to me he thanked God
for one thing.
He was not called back
until the canal was done.

"The Age of Wellington
fostered so many heroes of war,"
Esther, bonneted in black, was still talking,
though not to me, or anyone,
"and one great hero of peace."

She was still young. Beautiful.
And of great family.
She could ride and sing and write and draw
and none of it mattered.

She had prepared and carried through a monument
of obelisk, urn, heraldic crest,
words of her own making,
the motto of his family:
Give and Forgive.

Dear William:

You ask me to come back to Leeds and run for the vote again.
Being a friend and a man of honest mind, I'll tell you straight
why I will not return.

Better to be a merchant than a politician in these times.

Wolford farmers buy my axes.
Montague wives need cloth for quilts.
Labourers snort my whiskey.
Steamers raft my timber to the mills.

What's to gain in government?
With stale Bond Head and his Compact
Strachan and his church
bloody Gowan and his blackguards
where's the hustings can elect an honest man?

What's left of the Rebellion to belong to?
Durham and the Crown?
Folly to side with England in a county full of Irish.

Reform?
Secret lanterns only, after the Hogtown March.
Last month the Bytown came through
carrying rebels in chains:
a scraggly lot, sorry as pus-eyed potatoes.

The blockhouse no one needed in 1812
is going up now to hold back colonials.

I'll mind my store.
Not that I don't wish you luck if you're in the running.
I'll ride to Beverly to vote for you.

And I'll bring friends
and a rifle.

Your affectionate, loyal, obedient servant,
I remain,

John Kilborn, merchant,
Kilmarnock.

First Voice
All day the one task has been done
Under cloud in a drizzling mist,
And now it has taken on
A thick portentous glow,
The sun like a wizard alchemist
Sows everything gold as I sow...

Second Voice
We survived the Hunger of '46,
And the Hunger that followed, and exile,
Crossing in a fever ship
To the dreaded blue flag at Grosse Isle.

First
Gold that lifts and curves with the roll of the land;
Slivers of golden light at the forest's edge;
Gold in the grain, and the bag of grain; on clothes, and hand;
Uncannily skeined through the tangle of buckthorn hedge...

Second
We shivered next to naked in the snow,
Starved in the sheds of Montreal;
Then, through rain and heavier rain huddled like cattle
On an open deck on the Ottawa.

First
Gold over the roof of the house and a distant barn;
The whole sky melted gold, and the river's arm.

Second
As we passed the great fall of the Rideau,
We prayed to it, bade it cut its curtain through our woe.
We steamed the Long Reach into Wolford stillwater
Where we found our creek and walked it back to here.

Third Voice
This night when the round moon rides,
I will go down to the water and call on the wind to subside

And work up an evocation from this new hard land,
The way it is done in the old world at Columcille's strand,

And trust that hunger and suffering will have purged me
    enough I can see
Columba himself in a curragh drifting in across moonlight to
    me.

Some years the way deer do
Our families would split.
The men would go in groups to the lumber camps;
The children would stay with us
To watch over the animals
And weather the wind and snow as best we could.

We had plenty of time to think about their choice
And why so many went.
Habit, I suppose.
They'd been felling all their lives.
Pay perhaps. Men's company.
The need to prove themselves in one another's eyes.

The danger.
That ticklish pulse that flushes through your veins
When you peer off the rim of a cliff?
What better place to feel it than the bush
With all those blades and engines fit for mangling limbs
And trees crackling over everywhere,
Any one of them enough to crush a man.

And the drive.
Every season at the end
They'd build the sticks
Into huge timber rafts
And float them out with the floods.
Times they hit white water
They'd take the lot apart
And ride them through the rocks.

What surge on earth could match the thrill
Of biting bootnails into a log
Rolling and bucking like a beast alive
Through the lap and kick of the spray.

Or the feel of the final assembly
Floating straight at the tall ships
Right through the heart of the cove
With nothing but squared timbers floating
Far as the eye could see on every side
And raftsmen clapping and brawling,
Or dancing crazy to the fiddle on the logs.

Some of the men could come back after a drive
Settled enough to stay home the following year
Cutting ice or sledding quarried rock.
Others would be off again with the snow.
Occasionally, one would go and not come back.
A man would drown. Wherever the river
Chose to toss him out,
They'd carry him through the bush a hundred yards.
Dig him in. Bare heads. Make crosses on their chests.
Mutter fragments.
Mark the spot by nailing his boots to a tree.

I don't think it really matters where you lie
After you're dead.
Except maybe to the living
Until they die.

But if you have to be somewhere
It might as well be here

At Wolford beside the chapel
On the height of land.

Though Van Dusen's would be every bit as fine
With the river glinting slowly by the herds.

Or Merrickville with its plot so beautifully
Vined with Virgin's Bower.

There's a pit at the edge of the forest
Gouged just like a bed only grassed right over open
As if whoever was going
Thought the matter over
And settled for life.

The Indians, some say,
Buried their dead in the air.
Halfway to heaven, I'll suppose,
Though trees you'll notice when they decay
Crack and split and flail,
Use every means whatever
To come back home to earth.

The furnace that centres the eye of the foundry is cold.
The tongs are frozen open. The hammer lies flat.
The tannery stone is leaned so it will not roll.
A waterwheel turns to the hand, but only to demonstrate

How in the old mill's heyday a trundle moved
And meshed with a wallower to swirl a spindle, clatter
Buckets and belts about hoppers and grinders, powering men
    themselves
With the trusted force of simple flowing water.

Water still falls here. We hear it and are drawn out to it.
Around both sides of the island the surging tumble flows.
Down one bank, boathouse and ironworks still operate
In the shadow of Merrick's house and the dark of trees.

We follow the other channel and step across stone
That sent waves shimmering ten feet high in spring.
We make out the spot where we shouted one to one
And whisper of the mysteries of change.

The river that trickles off the Canoe Lake creeks
And slides with the slope of the soil down the tilt of the valley,
Thickened with swells and tributaries and the flood from the
    ocean lakes,
Will be ninety miles across when it puts out to sea.

Yet every inch of the way heron and pike live with intensity,
As people do who have married water in more ways than
    milling it.
Not only the Merricks, and By, and Harry McLean who
    constructed railways,
But the workers who coopered the barrels and quarried the mica
    pit.

Today's craftsman with his punch and a string of nails in his
   teeth.
The professor at his notes. The gardener so enthralled with her
   peonies
She kicks up a hummingbird's flutter with every breath;
The lift of her eye unearths a tiger lily's bugleburst of joy.

ARCHIVES

I

Beyond the glass, under the hill, the first blue
Splits ice past Hull to the cliff
Where Champlain points his astrolabe
Up the Grand River to the Inland Sea

Less than a mile from where the Colonel
In cocked hat and boots of a tighter age
Glowers over Bytown locks
And thinks of an enemy south.

II

Inside, walled in by racks and shelves
On one of many tables
Between the pad with my pen across it
And the box that I have emptied,

Embossed and sturdily bound, fossilized stiff
Except for some fuzz off the spine,
Is the Lockmaster's Journal Form Number 60
Where it is Kilmarnock and 1913.

November. Ice is coming in.
Time for tallying. Steamboats this year, 561
Sail and motor craft, 258. Seven rafts.
Lockages for pleasure, 403.

III

The pages turn like crisp dried hay
And fall to place firm flat.
Line by line the long script flows
Through date pilot cargo craft direction.

Noonan steers the Rideau King
Alternately up and down several times a page
With McCaw in his motor launch
Chugging up and down before or just behind.

Government tugs that go up empty
Come back carrying stone.
McGrath will have sold the Monitor
Before the Great War comes on.

Always the same hand, clear, serene,
All business with no omissions,
Few remarks, no signature,
Only a tax form in William Newsome's name.

For fifty seasons, William kept the lock
Or oversaw it kept by his brother John
From the time George Newsome was forced to give it up
After James – the original Maitland – yielded it.

Long lifetimes these, all with the one devotion
And this their Domesday Book.
Pondering on these spare notations,
I stretch my own capacities, catch

Glimmerings of figurehead and foam and rope I never saw,
And listen to the sounds I never heard
Of clinking chains on a crab
Or slamming of a stoplog into place.

I take in the smell of damp timber, reek of sedge,
Scent of pansies from the seeds from Plattsburg,
The Giant Trimardean in front of the blockhouse,
Mammoth Butterfly sown in a bed up the side,

And wonder how long it will be
Before anyone else makes the hours
To sift through the labyrinth
and pencil in on a slip RG43 1907,

How many years, if ever, before someone
Climbs to this room, extracts this journal and reads
To bring to the old lockmasters one more time
The gift of respondent breath.

I

Scrambling like a muskrat through the reeds,
He felt too small to be seen,
So he jumped and waved.

As it tipped Kilmarnock,
Chuffing up to Edmond's and Old Sly's,
It came so close he could read the

OLIVE.
Then the whistle blasted
Loud and long.

II

Like the original forwarders
Drummond and Tett and Dickinson
and Foster of later on,
he liked to captain his own ship.

When he had more than one,
he promised himself he would
love them all the same.

Piloting one or another
through the long stretch,
he would set to the tune
of the passing wharves
and the march of the cottage roofs
private praises in song.

The Lee was stubby and tough,
without fear.

Packed with dynamite,
she could butt like a flathead whale.

Double-engined Antelope could hammer too
and skip like the beast with its name.

Victoria was immense,
could carry two hundred passengers.
Peering from the top deck down
was like leaning from the bough of a tree.

With all three steamers going for the season
and fourteen crewmen scrambling,
he fretted so much
counting miles and weighing cargo,
eyeing gauges, measuring depths,
through the roar of fire
and the hiss of pressured steam
and the chunk and thump
of rods in the squealing shafts,
wallowing up to the neck
in oakum, putty, paint,
turpentine, tallow,
nails, bolts,
engine oil and grease,
sometimes it seemed he was steering
Victoria Antelope Lee together
all at once himself.

III

Nineteen twenty-eight.
He drifts in shallow water. The day is calm.
He is tempted to let go,
Focus on less and less,
Like an old clock winding down.

He follows his mood
Off the big lake
Up the channel
To Garden Island,
Studies in his mind
The clear depth of the water
As dimly plank on plank
The hull of the Rideau King
Shows through.

This afternoon he will do
What he set out to do.
Take the lumber to Portland.
Take the ice to Newboro.
Bring the apples to the Miekles and Mrs. Bates.

But now he drifts.
He hears a train whistle sounding
Beyond a line of trees.
He looks toward the sound
And catches a gleam from a motor car.

He thinks of the coming and the going
Of the steamboats
Through the timber boom
The mill era
And the fifty glorious years
That, short though they may be in the nation's life,
Had lasted most of his.

Neighbours

One morning he's at the farm before we are,
Smack at the heart of the driveway in his truck.
I have to swerve through a snowbank over the lawn
And when I come back walking he's on top

Half a head above me with his arms
And shoulders out the cab and the antenna
Crackling lightning in his hands. He makes
No greeting, simply looks at me and waits.

He blames his dogs, points a finger back
Beyond our shed, but one look at his jacket
Commando patched in orange and luminous
Tells me we're meeting at last the first of his kind.

Turns out he's a neighbour, farms the Rosedale
Sideroad half a mile northwest. He says
The wolves have killed some sheep. He says the wolves
Have killed a calf. Once we get him talking

He says more. He says our woods connect
With stands and copses right out of Montague
Into Goulbourn past the prison farm to Marlborough,
Miles of maple and pine and tangled scrub .

He says the dogs can run a wolf all day.
He follows with his radio and his truck
Until the wolf starts circling in a swamp.
Then he goes in.

I see the butt of his rifle on the seat
Dignified and quiet as a passenger.
He doesn't stay long. We don't invite him to.
He flicks the key on his engine and he's off
Chasing his dogs at somebody else's place.

***

That afternoon the snow is firm and fresh,
Perfect for tracks. We follow a fox through the ash.

We cross the triple bump of rabbit signs,
Spot the raccoon's mark, the squirrel's, the skunk's.

We come to where limbs and trunks have been gnawed bare,
Peeled to the dying flesh, and follow our guest

Where he draws us over a ridge with a furrowed track
Clean as a draftsman's line past rock and stump

To an ancient oak toppled, hollowed, warm,
Where a snowstained mark and a hole tell us we're far enough

And we wait and bow our heads and listen hard,
Matching our breaths to the wheeze of a prickly snore.

I flap with furious gestures marking the parallels
But Cathy misses the cue,
Curling off around the elm tree over a bump so sharp
Her bum's half off the seat.
She tilts a brow in feigned surprise
And bubbles a chuckle out,
Turning the wheel to jerk the mower down a depression
Up a swoop and off in dust,
Riding a runaway horse and loving it.

When Jamie takes his turn, he does it right.
He shears each line so straight you'd swear he was ruling it.
He holds the engine to a steady purr and where the corner's
    tight
Eases the tractor with deftness angled to accuracy.
Just as I'm wondering if he's got any humour in him
He lifts his eye and pops a little grin
And I recall how he read the manual with gravity,
Checked the oil with diligence, poked at wires and gears with
    the same intensity.
When the engine fired, you could hear his heart explode.

A woman we know, hearing we had maples,
Sailed in right away with advice on how to tap,
Figuring we'd need a hundred acres treed
To make it viable.
A second, more delicate,
Who'd never spent an hour in the cold,
Pressed palms and remembered sugaring bees
With jingling harness, pans and pails, and children licking taffy
    off the snow.

You, when I pointed to the square
And the sap flushing from it down the bark,
Simply tilted your head the way the rodent did
And pressed your tongue to the spot.
You called it good, and then moved on,
Content to leave sweetness pulling spring from earth,
Going where it should go,
Up through fibre into buds and dancing air.

This snow that fell in a soft swirled puff of flake,
Only a week ago crunched with a crisping sound.
Now it flicks at the sun with an oily gloss
And soon will be gone to air or underground.

If it goes down, the slope of the land suggests
It will spill through that nick in the sod, then nose out
A tunnel between the tractor and field rock.
It will slide under house, beneath woodyard, to sprout,

Not right away, nor even as water, through loam,
Through nodule and bulb. It will rise as lily and foxglove,
Profuse and scented and colourful, that Grandmother Campbell
– For years – stooped to and trowelled and patted in place with
    love.

She's known the woods too long
For us to think it's ignorance
That lets her walk in the trees
When the storm is up.

She goes out
Drawn magnetically
By the same force that pulls her
Steadily every day,

And will keep on calmly striding
To where a maple
Leans massively
Against its half-earthed root

With a desperate twist of its trunk
and a flurrying shudder of boughs.
She cannot help in the struggle
But will stay to watch it out.

Not everyone's way, we realize,
But her way to look straight
At the world in the world's terms,
And take all things in season,

Following snowprints gently over ice
Where deer have kicked through and sipped,
Sliding in summer through bees in the lilac
Listening to the whole bush hum.

Those of an age
are not like those of another.
Think of this river and birds.

Passenger pigeons were once so populous
groves would blacken under them.
Settlers would wallop
three at a sweep with clubs.

Now
here are the Lewises
greeting the sun with a spar
hoping to draw down a winged dream
lofty and wild

and the Bakers eyeing the marsh tower
horned with deadwood straggletop
where last year's pair of ospreys
nested their young.

"We were face deep in muck, I tell yez.
Jamie sez, spits out grit and sez to me,
'We'll have time to kiss the sun again
when the thing's over.'"

White haired, blue blazered,
with red at cap and chest,
he glared at the assembly
as if they were the enemy.
Then he said it again, more slowly.

" 'Time to kiss the sun again
when the thing's over.'
And now it's over
fifty years.

"How over, though, for
McGuigan with his knee
And Street who'll never see
and Quigg and Arthur deaf as stones?

"But most it's over now
for Jamie Vander Stock
abandoned in a field in Europe
lyin' under clay."

Old Crookback Silverhair
as I remember him,
before he twisted from the microphone
and tottered from the podium
out to a wash of light
and a flap of flags and drums.

MOTHER AND SON
MONTAGUE 1917

Standing at the fence
above the railway line
looking out at nothing
hair blown loose as hay
skirt ends writhing
like wool on a thorn

she could be seen from the road all day
but no one climbed up to her
or called out

she was in her grief
as in everything else
alone.

Melville, the loud
silly one,
as a matter of character
could not take his schoolbook seriously
and would not keep quiet about it
greeting Montcalm and Nelson
with cries of "Horse Manure, Cow Manure."
And naturally he kept on donkeying
while classmates posed
in their uniforms.
Of course he made up a song
and, prompted by fools,
bellowed it to the fairgrounds
complete with banjo and bones:
Balls to Smith's Falls
the Black-as-Coal
Trooper's Hole
to Hell.

Eventually, two

recruitment officers
with paper in hand
and a rifleman
marched to the field
and took him at his chores.

They left her to lead the horses
back to the barn herself.
She carried the harness into the shed
and hung it over the tree nail.
She left the plow where it was,
just as her son had angled it,
splitting the sod with a half blade
and a handle high in the air.

Your eye can come at him from anyone else's stall.
Like the point at the hub of a spinning top
He centres all.

Joy in his carvings echoes the lines in his face.
Firm and curved, they carry the same
Soft grace.

Though grained and clearly wooden, they seem not laboured at
    all,
Neither gouged nor shaved but sprung straight
From him whole.

They are polished and give off light, though a nick at the edge of
    one
Makes us think of vexations, handling, shelving, boxing out,
Boxing in,

And how each sale he makes must seem both severance and
    pride,
Like a father's on yielding a favoured son
To a bride.

We admire a bowl
So delicate no-one would eat from it
By a cup so sturdy only wooden wine could fill.

We feel the bond
Through a mother and child, an angel, a trio ascending
Carved in a single piece and mapleblond

With slab flat faces
That totally without features pack
More character than a living visage traces.

We look at the horse
With a mane so tight and thick
We swear we can hear it thunder the earth with a hoof,

As the trumpeter
Points a note through a matchstick
And blasts beyond South Mountain to the end of the universe.

This one alone's
Heavy as fieldstone.
Sturdy as a maul.
Everything in it's out of earth like a crop.
Straight as a plow's line here, curved like a fiddle there.
So womanly
It could give birth
Easy as a man's best cow.

Look at these log cabins.
Think what they celebrate.
  Snake Fence
  Windmill
  Lilac
  Hovering Hawks
All the things that make a farm a farm.

Every second Crazy Quilt you see
Has a family tied up in it,
Brother's pants, uncle's shirt,
Nobody left out.

Every fear, every loyalty in the county
Is on display, overlapped or
Side by side.

Thistles take hands with fleurs de lis
And spin with leprechauns.
Where else could you see
King Billy on a jackass
Parade with the Ku Klux Klan,

Or a Saint with his Book in front of a Church
Take a step to a Drunkard's Path?

Don't think the picture's all.
  colours and patterns of
  colours
  circles within
  circles
  revolve to make you giddy.
The squares sedate at the edge
Each get a speck of red
To make the whole line crackle like a fire.

Turkey Track's from Jasper.
Orange Peel's by –
You can read it –
Emmeline, thirteen years old.

Amberina
That covers half the wall?
My grandmother put that together
Thirty years ago.
It's good as new.

You should see her fold it in the chest
So tenderly you'd think it was thistledown.
The only one she keeps that way.
Usually, she's like my mother,
Wants to see things used,
Prefers the patterns open on a bed
Or riding on a clothesline
With all the colours flying in the wind.

He tractored slowly up from the end of his field,
gave at the top the high armed wave
of a man who has just retired,
then climbed down and started over
with his Lassie bouncing frisky at his knees.
I stopped my mower and met them near the road.

A wind was flailing grass against us,
blowing his white hair,
teasing the brim of my cap,
and we spoke loudly over it in bursts.

I praised the pace at which he'd cleared his brush
and he seemed pleased.
He waved his arm at the bared field and barked,
"Gas station." Then, with a sweep more to the west,
"Shopping mall." And way back along the treeline,
"Motor hotel." Finally, with a finger to his lips,
happy-eyed with his secret,
innocent as a child for all his years,
"Don't tell anyone."

* * *

Less than a year ago.
Yet, when he died so unexpectedly,
that ugly twist of fate
brought all his dreams
in one stroke
back to nothing.

We look at the black expanse
with its long earth scratches
and mounds of smouldered ash
and wonder what will happen to his plan.

How could his wife or son or daughter
imagine a first stride through the void
that must follow a man who was never still,
never silent, never without one of them
a step or two behind.

We, more distant,
will do much as we would have done
had they been less unfortunate,
think of plantings, restorations, gardens,
building our own dreams up from nothing
on our own side of the road.

* * *

For one long afternoon
the chunks and pieces of a life
are portioned and piled in front and back
and all around the gutted home.

Trucks and cartops gleam in a strip
a half a mile.
Strangers laughing and inquisitive mill with neighbours
through dressers, armchairs, tractors, tools, bric-a-brac,
so much stuff.
A man on a platform
in a cowboy hat
yodels through a microphone
as assistants scramble and yip
and a scribe at a computer taps the count.

Someone is selling hot dogs.

As someone else demonstrates
the workings of a bulldozer,
we remember it
pushing up till,

demolishing a stump,
clearing the field.

A saw set in a metal bench,
angular and ugly,
awkwardly uncomfortable on the lawn,
seems somehow less cold than it is,
more like a largeish pup.

Chirstmas ornaments
pulled one by one from a box
seem sadder
as they get lovelier.

Sad, too, for some of us,
the banal
Beware of Dog

and all the significance
tall grass cannot quite hide
of the huge bright yellow
SHELL
of a former station's sign.

What he does best
next to plowing and honking his horn
is talk.

There's a clip in his voice
bustles like water
bursting down a creek
sideslipping logs
skipping over rocks.

There's a rough scratching depth in it too,
a resonance of tractor engine
and great slow tires.

He keeps a reserve of humour
with a sense of weight
and substance like a good deep loam.

Like others who talk that well, he treasures his silences.
He can sit at a table an hour and not say a word
yet still take everything in like a long drag on a smoke.
Asked a question or prompted by a look,
he'll come back with something sensible
and speak it in his way.

Perpetually exhausting the strength of her white witchery
On the birth of cows and the naming of cows
And hexing the hundred demons from the stalls of cows,
She keeps no reserve for herself and suffers from allergy.

Affectionate cats, indifferent hay, pollen and dust
Take turns in attacking chest and eyes
Ears and throat with devilish accuracy,
Yet she scorns to take comfort in flight. She works where she
    must

As long as it needs to see a task done through.
No complaint. Each rasping breath
Builds spunk and hard earned tenderness.
Mornings first thing, chill in the air and clinging damp with
    dew,

If she hesitates,
It's less than the time it takes

To find a jacket's trailing second arm
To convince herself the farm appreciates all she does.
That her husband knows
And her children know
That in the great blazing centre of things God knows
As she zips up her coat and heads out straight for the barn.

There's more than the way he picks up a fork
And throws the hay in a great loose ball at a calf
Without even breaking stride
To tell us he's been at it all his life.

He says it himself on his way to milking.

Twice a day. Every day. With no holidays.
Not even the cows keep at it more than a dozen years.

Time to cut back. Trade the truck for a van.
Sell the less manageable lots.
Go from dairying to beef.
Sleep better.

He'll stroll more often down the path he has already mowed
To the bench at the side of the river
And with his wife for company
And the old dog at his feet
Let the rhythms of the waters build his soul,
Quiet as the longlegged heron peering through its reflection,
Or the cow in the margin of an ancient Holy Book,
Tranquil with the folded knees of patience,
Waiting for the slow Apocalypse.

FORTY-SEVEN

Forty-seven slides in from the darker side of the barn.
She wallows her Friesian ton through the flygrey air
Forestumped scythebacked slow down the holding bar
And lodges in mass dead still as an oldstone dolmen.
But the great rolled eye is not stone, nor the ear with its flick.
The muzzle is into the feed. The lolled tongue rasps as it rubs.
Once she's attached, her teats work milk down the tube
And splatter it into the glass. Her tail takes a swipe at a tick.

When the old girl's done with being done to,
She's unbarred up front and coaxed through,
Taking the corner so mincingly where it's wet
Even a shank her size seems delicate.
She plods then relaxed where light in an avenue flows
Into straw dung, and mud, and air, and the other cows.

Field Magic

Listening to runoff music where it glistens through the snow
We think perhaps to question waters, ask them where they're
    going to,
Then think better, simply stand by, hold our tongues and let
    them go.

Blocks of wood we've squared and piled up for the winter by the
    bridge
So primitive and natural its one log only edge to edge
May know, though they keep their silence. Elms and maples up
    the ridge

Murmur only with the wind what may be nothing anyway.
A slab of stone points backward upward to the pond we yester-
    day
Skated circling bold and bolder back right off the property

Furtively yet purposefully the way these ripples press the
    fenceline,
Undercut it to the river and farther rivers, past shorelines
America itself's been shifting since Paleozoic, pre-Cambrian.

It was the end of the run. August, mid-day.
Soaked with sweat, indifferent to droning flies,
I slowed to a walk coming out of the mudroad swamp
And eased my breath looking up at a deadtop's twist
And the heron lifting from it. Soundless, mysterious,
Greyer by far than the wood, it pointed its neck
And glided lingering swampward. Come again, its wing flapped.
Come again. Come again. And I thought that I would.

With the morning's mist, the welcoming was different.
A massive snake had wanted no part of me.
With its sudden head spearing in panic for grass,
It kept me poising, slowing my heel's descent
For one unforgettable throb as I elbowed the air and gaped
Into coils within coils unwinding in brilliant light.

Mid-run, in deep, shingles strewn on the ground,
A jamb laid flat and what was left of a wall
Rose up to declare a cabin was coming down,
Going back to the woods from which it had been wrenched.
Soft things go first, they said, and man was soft.
No good to rummage through leaves for a rusty pan
Or a squareheaded nail; no good to notice the mark
On a pine or the drift of a slope; these relics were nudging
In under. Vines would heap soon; and moss in a long
Slow wave. I would not find them again.

He's little more than a faun.
His tail's out stiff with fear.
His skip pretending confidence
Tells why he is here

So many miles from the deer yard
In so many inches of snow –
His mothering world has kicked him off,
He has nowhere else to go.

He runs up the road, which is folly;
And crosses it, which is worse;
But he knows where the wire is down,
Speeds up on a better course,

Slants off veering wisely
And takes split rails in a bound
To where river and space and acres of shrub
Make the best deer country around.

I am always stirred
At the sight of the tracks crisscrossing.
No wonder.

Their seasonal rounds
Loop paths we amble together
All year long.

Their counterpointings, side by side
Or step over stepping, match
How we pair up;

How you gauge
The light off a spring fern while I conjure
Its name;

How you aim your lens
At a polypore as I
Study bark.

Always in winter
We look for the foxes flitting
Against the snow,

Hoping to glimpse
If only an instant this image
Of who we are.

But they are crafty,
More likely to be where we don't look,
Behind us,

Nostrils poised, ears up,
Conning with inquisitive respect
Through eyes like pins,

Trying to make out precisely
A tantalizing shadow of themselves
That puzzles them.

PRICKLY ASH

I

In love with green shadows
subtlety of hepatica
trout lily, trillium
we thread our way
through the margin of the wood
and do it gracefully
but for the ash
scratching our arms
puncturing our hands –
prickly ash –
sturdy, supple, clumped.

We insist on our
shoulder to shoulder
of room
and down it
where it blocks us,
lop it to stubs,
flailed off shreds,
amputated leavings piled in humps;
when it comes back in shoots
we hack at it again;
when it rains
we probe with care
under the lowest thorns
and pull it up by the roots.

II

The predicament at the meadow's edge is different.
There ash extends too wide for easy cutting.

For a time we plotted our future forest out,
Trimmed back any thorn bush that grew by a basswood stem.

And yet we've seen a maple twice our height
Shade out a ring of dead-stick ash.

And a layer of fresh green ash boughs
Protecting groundhugged oak.

If we leave the ash just as it is
Will the friendlier mass of forest flourish again?

Neither ash nor maple is saying.

III

From way deep in
where the oldest giants
peckerdrilled, coonholed
and majestic
tower
we sense on a whisper of wind
that answers will come of wisdom

a wisdom we will learn
from the lift and fall of each day's sun
tumble of waters
animals insects birds
and the spill of the stars

a wisdom we will earn
by being where we are
waiting
watching while we wait.

1. ONE

One day there's one toppled across the path
broken in great thick chunks,
so aromatic it seems an eternal spring,
as if it were not part of the forest at all
but an entry to Paradise.

We recognize it, though.
So well we can pace out a length
we remember as height
to find fur in a ball and packed earth.

Apart from shifting a topbough
that pressures a sapling's lift
we leave it just as it fell
angled across our trail
going its own way down
the long descent to soil
by fungus and mite and moss
beak and claw and rain
and our own unconscious footfalls
for as long as we come through.

Earthdark concave
off the roots.

Above, an oval centred black
where a bough twisted out
maybe ten years ago.

Between them
on the outer shell
a runway up the grey
clawed clean to reddish underbark.

A home
for somebody.
But is it built down with the raccoon,
or up with the porcupine?

We've seen the triple spreadprint of the one,
quills and dirtheaps of the other
and signs of squirrels, rabbits,
a returning fox.

With dusk
will come rustlings, leaf flicks,
scratches and skitterings,
perhaps a ruffled hooting
owl to owl.

3. BASSWOOD

So thick
that taking hands
and spreading arms in a curve
we cannot make it halfway round.

So tall
scanning with glasses
up through a tangle of boughs
we mistake its leaves
for maple leaves

before we read the secret
at its base.
For this prodigious trunk
has six tight smaller trunks
thrust up in a circle around it –
each with wide curved leaves.

The basswood is less a tree
than a colony of trees
sprouted from a central post.

A full thick specimen
is a magnificence
of mass and soaring pillars
densely packed with shadows
and drooping clumps of green.

Even a severed trunk
lopped ragged as a crater's rim
can keep its flock attending round its girth
fresh and supplely waving in a ring.

Eventually a ring alone can stand
with its central core
so much an emptiness

it lures us sinking earthward
to thumbnail blackened fibres
under moss.

4. OAK

Where pondhollow drops to creekbed
and fence wires tumble with nightshade,
two towering oaks stand
ninety feet in the air
hulking wide.

Titans sturdy as cliffs
and splendidly contradictory,
they measure a rooty swampstep
to hover hugely skyward.

Headstrong as summer bears,
they pack their shapes
in twists and nudgings
bluntly independent of the lines
of other trees.

They shed twigs and barkbits always,
yet where the true limbs split
hold them dangling
by the grey outer bark
for days and weeks and months
reluctant to let them go.

5. MAPLE

We misconceive their upper crests
to be ethereal, pristine
tufts of breezy light
but even a midsized branch
snapped off upended
smashed against the shrubbery
shows
lichens rough as barnacles,
galls, scars,
furrows,
twists of woodgrain,
bruising crushing weight.

6. ELM

If there's a tall pole
lancing through the understorey
or flattened grey in the leaves
it's probably an elm.

It will be topped out branchless
springy shaggy taut
so solid there seems nothing wrong with it
but for the punkdry
rotting in the root.

Its outer edge repels
the first bite of a sawblade
though once you're into it
it cuts out firm and true.
Every grain line comes up
sturdy, clear.
Each forearm's length
feels heavy as stone
and packs with a knock
proclaiming
even when dead
it is a tough tough wood.

A sliver of nailflicked bark
reveals the beetle mark
to call it worse than dead
call it diseased and dying out,

so even the push of a sapling
seems now sad
and sad
all through the grove
what would have been beautiful otherwise
the rustling of the upper leafage
wavering in the breeze.

7. CEDAR

At first they seem like sufferers
trapped in shadows.
Their flayed bark shreds in strips,
their dead limbs tangle like grey bones.
The only green about them seems
the green of undermoss
and tips the squirrels have nipped from overhead
to straggle in the duff.

But the little tips contain
hordes of russet seedlings;
the shadows come from upper branches'
waves of evergreen;
bones and raggedness
taken from a distance
become a smoothswept
swirl of trunks
crisscrossed with a symphony of lines
visual at first
then heard with concentration
as the wind sweeps through
with the heaving hissing sigh
of cedars firm a hundred years
still stretching.

They are versatile, persistent,
patient in their spread,
sprigging inchtall delicate
out of red cored pulp;
spindling headlong down hill
over boulders into peat;
angling to climb a hump and over
aromatic, resinous,
thickbrushed root to crown.

8. TROUBLE

When we see the shavings under
we know a tree's in trouble.
The pilleated woodpecker
drills its holes
– huge gaping squared off cavities –
only where ants
are tunneling.

Lightning takes a tree
down faster.
And there's a quarter mile of rubble
where the cyclone swooped.

Fire's another snapping jaw.
And there are slower deaths.

Too much snow.
Too little.

Deer that browse at one height.
Rabbits and mice at another.

Bear claws.
Fungus.
Weevils.

Vines that insinuate
entwine
and knot in tangles.

Porcupines.
Beavers.

Mostly
one another.

Somehow some survive
singly, paired
in margins
clumps groves forests
keeping precarious balance.

Just when you think
you've got a corner
of the woodlot
mapped precisely in your mind
you come across a tree
you realize you'd missed

always so significant
in size or twist or lean
you wonder how you could have overlooked
the solemn solid sureness
of its dance.

You begin to look for others
and you find them.

Here a gaunt strider
splits dendritically
into a pocket of air.

Here an old patriarch
nine tenths gone
sideswipes to brace up
an elegant scarf of limbs.

Here a struggler
shifts for light
and guides the eye to more trees
here and here and here.

Though they shift in every wind,
change shape at each new
slanting of the sun,
they are not lost.
They know everything around them.
Know what has come

and is to come.
Whatever we may not know,
they know who they are.

New growth rising
where the land was cleared
already is coming back to
mystery and charm.
The same is true of wedges
cut for access into the maplebush.
Still the original uncleared forest
holds the deepest truths.
Under its thicker moss
the dip and roll of the glacial till
seems more clearly marked.
Roots writhe higher somehow
encouraging foxes to burrow
and sow the earth with bones.
Rotted logs smell funkier
and block the nostrils like incense.
Nettles and mushrooms conspire with thorns
to conjure a headier dew.
The dead giants lift shoulders
and preside
like pillars marking limits
keeping the primal shaping of a shrine.

One with bared running grain
has the look of a dry beached log.
It opens inward womblike in a long slit
slanted to share the thrust of its trunk.
Its smoothed outer margin
spirals like the ulna of an arm.
Its top diverges hollowed
through a blackrimmed core
to funnel air like a woodpipe
breathe with old composure
probe with an invitation
pointed like a spyglass into heaven.

After all the other birds
Have dropped off one by one
The wood thrush shapes the sunset
To its final perfect turn

With a flute piece piped streamsilvery
Lush as the greenwood's depth.
I crept out one time to look at it
But only made it stop.

Now I stand at the margin and listen
As it trills a touch of daring
Into all the shyest ones,
Coaxing the groundhog up from its den, steering

The cottontails out to the lawn
And the doe to the rim of the clearing
To browse a last thin stretch of sun back to mist
And the dark where the thrush is singing.

Studying feathery snowlines of crystals over shadow
On a day so cold even the rock seems frozen,
We find tucked away the familiar sawtoothed edge
Of the tiny triple leaf.

We've seen them run green in November,
Prolific in places they'll be
When the first soft mud comes slushing
Back to the air in spring.

In flowering time,
Their white and gold array
Will blaze in patches so thick
We'll be pressed to find a spot to place a foot.

Meadow creepers, they will storm hills if inclined,
Dive deep woods, percolate tall grass
Huddled so low you can find them after mowing
Still deftly succulent red under leaf.

They are wild, will not be cropped,
Mischievously keep berries nothing but miniscule
That no-one could hoard in a bowl,
Self-willed, fragile, too delicate almost to taste,

Except by the few who love them enough
To become like them. Patient. Subtle. Willing to
Dip small centred; concentrate;
Cherish the elixir; bear the stain.

Where the shrubbery thickened and wedged into deeper dark
I caught the lifted arc
From tangle and rot of a muscular twist of tree
And marvelled at how punkwood void of bark
Could shrug off its mortality.

"It's not dead – look again," you told me.
And I looked up to see
The basswood knot and burst from a junction fit
With a joyous thrust of green, alive, as much your tree
As if you had planted it.

So once you took a dream that I had loved
But thought had faded
And breathing through it flushed it as a coal
Blown to flame again, tall crested
Fierce and full.

Twenty years together and still more ways to love,
Profounder, fresher, better ways, more sensible.
Your latest kiss is subtler than the globeflower
It took us half a day to realize was there.

We'd long since seen the whalebone hump of rock,
The gentle spread of lilies on the pond,
Our second then our third bright logwarmed turtle
And seven balls of unsubmerging duck.

We sat at our shaded height so quietly so long
The heron we'd scared forgot us and came back.
It wafted over cattails and watercress aimed at a stump
And in its reflection grazed a spray of stars.

Binoculars proved stars to be our buttonbush.
Aquatic, yes, yet sundrawn substantially green
And triply globed with rough tight nuggetfruit,
Clusters of white corolla and outer spheres

Of goldtipped pins so intricately exuberant,
So soft and deftly burning, only the brush of your tongue
And all the complexity of tenderness it tells
Is balanced more adroitly with more infinite messengings.

Topping your packet of photographs, the best of them all.
Indian Pipe, deceptively bland as clay,
Spurts in knock-kneed clusters, droops in a frothing of bells.
It has charmed my eye and picked at my mind all day.

I have leaned on knee and elbow, made ritual turns,
Stood in quiet observance like a pagan votary
Reflectively haunting himself over ash in an urn
Or a fossilized relic of bark from a sacred tree,

And do not know why. Perhaps it is sentiment,
Knowing how much you care for your camera.
You've got the exposure right, and that is significant,
For harsh mixed light was vexing the woods that day.

Sharpness of colour and line, or the flow of shapes
May be what pleases the eye; and a little caprice can whip
The roll of belltops into a prancing of sheep
Or thirty frolicsome maids at a bonneted skip.

Perhaps it is the flower itself that enchants,
The tenacity, the impudent audacity with which it flaunts
Its scaly bracts uniquely through mere greenery ,
Spurning the ease of sunlight for the decay of roots.

Or perhaps because, sentiment again, beside
The photograph rests Daniel's first book, so new
I can see the print of his thumb and feel the pride
With which he read from it, throbbing through
Injustice, severance, death like a great bell in a cathedral
For Nina, just as strong,
Who had endured as much as long,
Absorbing like the vault of a rosewindowed arch the ringing
    ringing ringing of the bell.

We knew them first by a redness in the bark,
The way they had of splaying from the trunk,
Then ovate leaves and nubbing twigs, and wind dance, each
 flower
A pink haze flushing through a five-point bed of white;

At last, the fruit rounding and riding profusely
Through thicket and hedge and fenceside, everywhere we
 looked,
Wanton in clusters. Apples twisted at eye level
And scattered abundant. Some grew heavy and thumped to
 grass.

Hundreds bubbled skyward out of reach.
Always a firm coquettish few at handstretch
Demanded a touch of fondling in the plucking,
A curve of the flesh to the applecurve before they would give.

Yellow or green or russet cornered, they leaned to tartness.
Even when bagged, they held to feistiness.
A ripple as light as a hand's through water
Would thunder them softly like vanishing hooves of deer.

Cut, submerged, and boiled, they keep their odour.
Their mash and scum stay applelike. Their warm and subtle
Threads of steam burgeon full of quality.
As the spooned mass thickens to a pendant globe,

It centres and pulls at something deep in us.
Tomorrow we will pick from a tree a little
Farther out where nature is taking more
Of the pasture back a little faster. The next
Day after that, we'll forage deeper still.

KILMARNOCK MEDITATIONS

I

Though he's been gone some years
I still talk to my dog,
Call him the playful names
I used to shout as I jogged,
Even look past my shoulder
As I always did if he lagged.

II

Beginning with whatever ends they find
  Remains of some abandoned nest
    Moulded feathers long past use
      Whatever dead or dying thing
        They can drag in a beak
        Through a hole to the dark
      Whether straw or mud or dung
    With infinite chitter and fuss
  My swallows building their box nest
Wind my end through my beginning.

III

We are all born,
Will all die.
Not much is certain.
But I am certain
Wherever we have come from
Is where we will return.

IV

Earth did not want to give it up
Where I dug it out of the soil
The bone, perhaps the pelvic bone,
Of a scattered animal
With moss growing over it
And pockholes drilling into it
Drawing it
One worm's width at a time
Closer to air.

And I recall the grass
Twined and knotted stubbornly
Over a skull
That now rests comfortably
Stretched along a board above the hearth
Poising a pair of orifices
So balanced vertically attentive
We almost see brown eyes within them
Move.

V

With a twist of a screwdriver
And a light fist's press against the wood
I lifted the roof of last year's box
And you pulled out the squared off nest
To find
Four eggs
Small whitish
One topped
With the sharp black star
Of opening.

VI

Between rolled leaves
On a green limb
A fluffed embalmment
Tight as a spadix
In a spathe.

VII

A living bird gave up the egg in the nest upon the table.
A mammal marrowed the bone in the skull upon the mantel.

What bird, which animal
We cannot tell

Though I have been tempted to put one question to test
By climbing thorns to a screeching kingbird's nest.

I have straddled a split rail fence with binoculars
Narrowed to the curve of a woodchuck's ear.

   And yet I sense despite this fidgeting
     That I do not want
       To know

   Would rather have remnants settling
     Passive as water's slideslant
       In a hollow

   Until they have gathered enough
     To weather a trough
       And flow

Flow the way stars do
So many up there on a clear night
We cannot imagine heaven

Holding anything but all of them

The way a summer field holds birds
Barn swallows veering everywhere
Bobolinks gurgling through pasture
Catbirds perched in the thicket edge
Mockingbirds beaked straight up in ecstasy
From ground leaves to limbtops
Bouncing back all song.

The way in deeper woods
Above the fungus shelf
The severings, the drill holes
The gaping hollowed corewood
Of even the oldest trees,
Ever sturdily skyward
Through spreading topmost limbs
Verdure spills triumphant,
And down deep down
With the earthmost roots
And the shaggiest moss
The simple vital lifting
Of the supple maple stem
Knows its strength and flourishes
In a billowing mass of green.

Near the mudmarks where the fox skims brush,
Skirts fence and angles west, where the soil begins
To smell a little more like moss and the shadows start,
We find the plow, and will keep finding it.
How can it be here, we'll wonder every time,
Not barned or yarded like any other implement,
But locked in alien trees and tangle and rock,
Neighboured by rodents alone, humbled absolutely beneath
The hollow and shag of a barreling, toppled bough.
Transom to sock, it still packs a sturdy weight
And keeps the russeted look of an honest labourer.
Its metal where you knuckle at it hums
And almost rings. Like a fang all eager,
Its blade still tapers downcurled, and yet it bites
No grassroot, thrusts no heaving sillion, plows
Only the air when the wind squeezes through twigs,
Plows only a flurry of thoughts at the back of the mind
Scavenging like gulls behind a furrower.

A man stoked and bellowed fire to forge this iron.

A man used it to till his clearing to crop.

Who was it buried it here like something that made him
  ashamed?

We scrabble and pry. We kneel and squint at a foundry mark.
Percival; the name suggests an ancient knight.
An opera's Easter. To me, the character in my novel,
Long unpublished, still loose pages in a box.

Well, Mister Percival, how do we make amends?
Shall we bring in a horse or a tractor, draw in a dozen friends
To lift you or drag you out through the brush past the fence
  to the clearing?

Should we dump you by the shed with the dead pump and two
   sleds and the wagon
To wallow through snowdrifts or grass as the seasons play
   pitch and toss?
Or invite you right into the house, a tidied and painted ornament,
To scratch at floorboards in the tiny north window's well?

We're likely to do what is easiest and seems right.
Follow your current example. Plow nothing. Leave you alone.
Let the flux of the countering powers that blasted you
   out of the quarry,
Melted and battered you down to this shape, dragged
You through grit, uncoupled and left you with nettles
   and leafmould,
The twists that pull and rub us all unendingly,
Let them have the say in your fate's unravelling fix.
They may keep you quiet here nestled in soil and shrubbery
For raccoons and rabbits, for us, to chance upon
Or grow to expect like an old friend. They may dig you out,
Clear the bush. The woods have moved in books
And can in life, through fire or storm or pestilence
Or steady slow attrition limb by limb .
I think of the fault line further back in the scrub
And dream of a wilder fate, an owlish night
With a mythic Plowman striding the air like a cloud,
Finding you out, hefting your weight in his hands,
Hitching you to the horse of the earth, cutting
Deep, way deep through soil and crust and bedrock
To plow the horizon through and sow the stars.

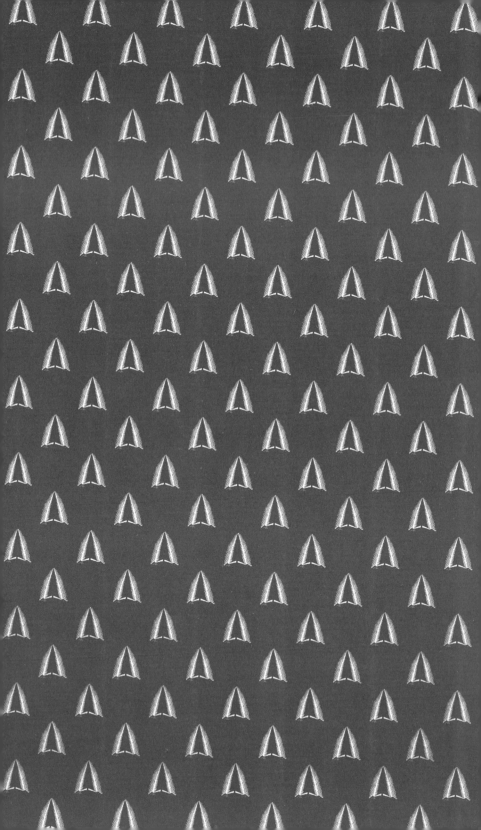